UNDER ALL SILENCES

SHADES OF LOVE

UNDER ALL SILENCES
SHADES OF LOVE

An Anthology of Poems Selected by

RUTH GORDON

HARPER & ROW, PUBLISHERS

Under All Silences: Shades of Love
An Anthology of Poems Selected by Ruth Gordon

Copyright © 1987 by Ruth I. Gordon
Printed in the U.S.A. All rights reserved.
Designed by Bettina Rossner
1   2   3   4   5   6   7   8   9   10
First Edition

Library of Congress Cataloging-in-Publication Data
Under all silences.

"A Charlotte Zolotow book."
Summary: An anthology of poems about love by E. E.
Cummings, Rainer Maria Rilke, William Butler Yeats, and
other authors.
1. Love poetry.   2. Children's poetry.   [1. Love
poetry]   I. Gordon, Ruth I., 1933–   .
PN6110.L6U46 1987   808.81'9354   85-45845
ISBN 0-06-022154-2
ISBN 0-06-022155-0 (lib. bdg.)

To my Father and the memory
of my Mother—
Now, silently voiceless,
Your words resound

ACKNOWLEDGMENTS

Every effort has been made to trace the ownership of all copyrighted material and to secure the necessary permissions to reprint these selections. In the event of any question arising as to the use of any material, the editor and the publisher, while expressing regret for any inadvertent error, will be happy to make the necessary correction in future printings. Thanks are due to the following for permission to reprint the copyrighted materials listed below:

YAMABE NO AKAHITO: "I wish I were close . . . ," from Kenneth Rexroth, *One Hundred Poems from the Japanese*. All rights reserved.

YOSANO AKIKO: "Black hair . . ." and "Not speaking of the way . . . ," from Kenneth Rexroth, *One Hundred More Poems from the Japanese*. Copyright © 1974, 1976 by Kenneth Rexroth. Reprinted by permission of New Directions Publishing Corp.

MAYA ANGELOU: "In Retrospect," from *And Still I Rise* by Maya Angelou. Copyright © 1978 by Maya Angelou. Reprinted by permission of Random House, Inc.

ANONYMOUS, Egyptian hieroglyphic text: "I wish to paint my eyes . . . ," reprinted by permission of Schocken Books Inc. from *A Book of Women Poets*, edited by Aliki Barnstone & Willis Barnstone. Copyright © 1980 by Schocken Books Inc.

ANONYMOUS, Egyptian hieroglyphic text: "So small are the flowers of Seamu . . . ," Ezra Pound, *Love Poems of Ancient Egypt*. Copyright © 1962 by Noel Stock. Reprinted by permission of New Directions Publishing Corp.

ANONYMOUS, Indian Sanskrit: "Her eyes in sleep . . ." and "Living here . . . ," from *The Peacock's Egg*. Copyright © 1977 by Columbia University Press. Published by North Point Press and reprinted by permission. All rights reserved. Translated by W. S. Merwin and J. Moussaieff Masson.

ANONYMOUS, Japanese: "Like the tides' flood . . . ," from Kenneth Rexroth, *One Hundred More Poems from the Japanese*. Copyright © 1974, 1976 by

CONTENTS

A NOTE TO THE READER

The poems in this collection were selected because they describe the many shades of love, from the first attraction through deepening affection, passion, and the search beyond the physical person and world for pure beauty—to (for a rare few) the ultimate knowledge of a supreme being.

We can be struck dumb by strong emotions, the emotions felt in the many stages of love. But in these poems our feelings find release, for they express the love that is the voice under all silences.

UNDER
ALL
SILENCES

SHADES
OF
LOVE

The First Time Ever I Saw Your Face

The first time ever I saw your face,
I thought the sun rose in your eyes,
And the moon and stars were the gift you gave
To the dark and empty skies, my love,
To the dark and empty skies.

The first time ever I kissed your mouth,
I felt the earth move in my hand,
Like the trembling heart of a captive bird
That was there at my command, my love,
That was there at my command.

The first time ever I lay with you
And felt your heart beat close to mine,
I thought our joy would fill the earth
And last till the end of time, my love,
And last till the end of time.

Ewan MacColl (b. 1915)

Love Song to a Stranger

How long since I've spent a whole night
in a twin bed with a stranger,
his warm arms all around me?
How long since I've gazed into dark eyes
that melted my soul down
to a place where it longs to be?
All of your history
has little to do with your face.
You're mainly a mystery
with violins filling in space.

You stood in the nude by the mirror
and picked out a rose
from the bouquet in our hotel,
and lay down beside me again.
And I watched the rose
on the pillow where it fell.
I sank and I slept in a twilight
with only one care,
to know that when day broke
and I woke you'd still be there.

The hours for once
they passed slowly, unendingly by,
like a sweet breeze on a field.

Your gentleness came down upon me
and I guess I thanked you
when you caused me to yield.
We spoke not a sentence
and took not a footstep beyond
our two days together
which seemingly soon would be gone.

Don't tell me of love everlasting
and other sad dreams,
I don't want to hear.
Just tell me of passionate strangers
who rescue each other
from a lifetime of cares.
Because if love means forever
expecting nothing returned,
then I hope I'll be given
another whole lifetime to learn.

Because you gave to me
oh so many things,
it makes me wonder
how they could belong to me.
And I gave you only my dark eyes
that melted your soul down
to a place where it longs to be.

Joan Baez (b. 1941)

———

3

Mathematics of Love

The links are chance, the chain is fate,
Constricting as Hephaistos' net
Which to the smiles of gods betrayed
Two bodies on a single bed,
So tightly knit, the truth was plain:
One multiplied by one is one.

Subtracting lovers who retort
That what chance coupled, choice can part
(As if mere effort could relax
The clutches of a paradox)
At last to their amazement find
Themselves the dwindled dividend,

Deep in that hell where Don Juan
Knows he has added names in vain
Since all the aggregate is lost
To him, not widowed but a ghost,
While those bereaved of one possess
A minus greater than his plus.

True love begins with algebra,
Those casual actors x and y,
Nonentities whose magic role
Is to turn nothing into all,
To be and not to be, to mate:
The links are chance, the chain is fate.

Michael Hamburger (b. 1924)

The Apple

You have enslaved me with your lovely body;
You have put me in a kind of prison.
Since the day we parted,
I have found nothing that is like your beauty.
So I comfort myself with a ripe apple—
Its fragrance reminds me of the myrrh of your breath,
Its shape of your breasts, its color
Of the color that used to rise to your cheeks.

Judah Halevi (c. 1075–1141)
Translated from the Hebrew
by Robert Mezey

Silent Noon

Your hands lie open in the long fresh grass,—
   The finger-points look through like rosy blooms:
   Your eyes smile peace. The pasture gleams and glooms
'Neath billowing skies that scatter and amass.

All round our nest, far as the eye can pass,
   Are golden kingcup-fields with silver edge
   Where the cow-parsley skirts the hawthorn-hedge.
'Tis visible silence, still as the hour-glass.

Deep in the sun-searched growths the dragon-fly
Hangs like a blue thread loosened from the sky:—
   So this wing'd hour is dropt to us from above.
Oh! clasp we to our hearts, for deathless dower,
This close-companioned inarticulate hour
   When twofold silence was the song of love.

Dante Gabriel Rossetti (1828–1882)

Hiding Our Love

Never believe I leave you
From any desire to go.
Never believe I live so far away
Except from necessity.
After a whole day of separation
Still your dark fragrance clings to my skin.
I carry your letter everywhere.
The sash of my dress wraps twice around my waist.
I wish it bound the two of us together.

Do you know that we both conceal our love
Because of prior sorrow, superstitious fear?
We are two citizens of a savage era
Schooled in disguises and in self-command,
Hiding our aromatic, vulnerable love.

Carolyn Kizer (b. 1925)

Based on a poem
by the Emperor Wu-Ti

Not speaking of the way,
Not thinking of what comes after,
Not questioning name or fame,
Here, loving love,
You and I look at each other.

Yosano Akiko (1878– 1942)
Translated from the Japanese
by Kenneth Rexroth

I wish I were close
To you as the wet skirt of
A salt girl to her body.
I think of you always.

Yamabe No Akahito
(8th century)
Translated from the Japanese
by Kenneth Rexroth

I wish to paint my eyes,
so if I see you, my eyes will glisten.
When I approach you and see your love,
you are richest in my heart.
How pleasant this hour is!
May it extend for me to eternity.
Since I have lain with you
you have lifted my heart high.

Anonymous, Egyptian hieroglyphic text
(c. 1500 B.C.)
Translated by Willis Barnstone

Among Iron Fragments

Among iron fragments and rusty dreams
I found you

lost in my astonished hands:
is this your face, your shoulders; this, the hair of night?

Dark flame and sleepy mouth
the years have forgotten your eyes

they rose up around you
with the sharpness of spikes

the fine, white dust above you
in winds that rose and died.

I found you
my wounded face in the wind and my arms open wide.

Tuvia Ruebner (b. 1924)
Translated from the Hebrew
by Robert Friend

Thank you, my dear

You came, and you did
well to come: I needed
you. You have made

love blaze up in
my breast—bless you!
Bless you as often

as the hours have
been endless to me
while you were gone.

Sappho
(7th century B.C.)
Translated from the Greek
by Mary Barnard

A Secret Kept

A girl brought me into the house of love,
A girl as pure and perfect as Abigail,
And taking off her clothes, she revealed a body
So dazzling, it beggared comparison.
Her light shining in the darkness made everything tremble,
The hills began dancing like rams.
"O Lord," I thought, "our secrets will be discovered,"
But she reached back at once with her powerful hands
And covered us both with her long black hair,
And once again it was night.

Judah al-Harizi (c. 1170–1235)
Translated from the Hebrew
by Robert Mezey

747

There's a strange frenzy in my head,
of birds flying,
each particle circulating on its own.
Is the one I love *every*where?

Rumi (1207–1273)
Translated from the Persian
by John Moyne and Coleman Barks

As We Are So Wonderfully Done
with Each Other

As we are so wonderfully done with each other
We can walk into our separate sleep
On floors of music where the milkwhite cloak of childhood
    lies

O my lady, my fairest dear, my sweetest, loveliest one
Your lips have splashed my dull house with the speech of
    flowers
My hands are hallowed where they touched over your
    soft curving.

It is good to be weary from that brilliant work
It is being God to feel your breathing under me

A waterglass on the bureau fills with morning . . .
Don't let anyone in to wake us.

Kenneth Patchen (1911—1972)

In Retrospect

Last year changed its seasons
subtly, stripped its sultry winds
for the reds of dying leaves, let
gelid drips of winter ice melt onto a
warming earth and urged the dormant
bulbs to brave the
pain of spring.

We, loving, above the whim of
time, did not notice.

Alone. I remember now.

Maya Angelou (b. 1928)

Sappho to Eranna

I want to flood you with unrest,
want to brandish you, you vine-clasped staff.
Like dying I want to pierce through you
and pass you on like the grave
to the All: to all these waiting things.

Rainer Maria Rilke (1875–1926)
Translated from the German
by Edward Snow

Wild Nights—Wild Nights!
Were I with thee
Wild Nights should be
Our luxury!

Futile—the Winds—
To a Heart in port—
Done with the Compass—
Done with the Chart!

Rowing in Eden—
Ah, the Sea!
Might I but moor—Tonight—
In Thee!

Emily Dickinson (1830–1886)

Black hair
Tangled in a thousand strands.
Tangled my hair and
Tangled my tangled memories
Of our long nights of love making.

Yosano Akiko (1878–1942)
Translated from the Japanese
by Kenneth Rexroth

On a Night of the Full Moon

I

Out of my flesh that hungers
and my mouth that knows
comes the shape I am seeking
for reason.
The curve of your waiting body
fits my waiting hand
your breasts warm as sunlight
your lips quick as young birds
between your thighs the sweet
sharp taste of limes.

Thus I hold you
frank in my heart's eye
in my skin's knowing
as my fingers conceive your flesh
I feel your stomach
moving against me.

Before the moon wanes again
we shall come together.

II

And I would be the moon
spoken over your beckoning flesh
breaking against reservations
beaching thought
my hands at your high tide
over and under inside you
and the passing of hungers
attended, forgotten.

Darkly risen
the moon speaks
my eyes
judging your roundness
delightful.

Audre Lorde (b. 1934)

This morning I will not
Comb my hair.
It has lain
Pillowed on the hand of my lover.

Kakinomoto No Hitomaro
(7th century)
Translated from the Japanese
by Kenneth Rexroth

We were together
Only a little while,
And we believed our love
Would last a thousand years.

Ōtomo No Yakamochi
(718–785)
Translated from the Japanese
by Kenneth Rexroth

Her eyes in sleep
afterward

her body my love

sounds she uttered then
without meaning

yet not meaningless

my heartbeat even now
echoing them.

Anonymous, Indian Sanskrit
(10th century or earlier)
Translated from the Sanskrit
by W. S. Merwin
and J. Moussaieff Masson

Waiting

My love will come
will fling open her arms and fold me in them,
will understand my fears, observe my changes.
In from the pouring dark, from the pitch night
without stopping to bang the taxi door
she'll run upstairs through the decaying porch
burning with love and love's happiness,
she'll run dripping upstairs, she won't knock,
will take my head in her hands,
and when she drops her overcoat on a chair,
it will slide to the floor in a blue heap.

Yevgeny Yevtushenko (b. 1933)
Translated from the Russian
by Robin Milner-Gulland and Peter Levi, S.J.

Bright House

It is a bright house;
not a single room is dim.

It is a house which rises high
on the cliffs, open
as a lookout tower.

When the night comes
I put a light in it,
a light larger than the sun and the moon.

Think
how my heart leaps
when my trembling fingers
strike a match in the evening.

I lift my breasts
and inhale and exhale the sound of love
like the passionate daughter of a lighthouse keeper.

It is a bright house.
I will create in it
A world no man can ever build.

Fukao Sumako (1893–1974)
Translated from the Japanese
by Kenneth Rexroth and Ikuko Atsumi

II
from Twenty-One Love Poems

I wake up in your bed. I know I have been dreaming.
Much earlier, the alarm broke us from each other,
you've been at your desk for hours. I know what I
    dreamed:
our friend the poet comes into my room
where I've been writing for days,
drafts, carbons, poems are scattered everywhere,
and I want to show her one poem
which is the poem of my life. But I hesitate,
and wake. You've kissed my hair
to wake me. *I dreamed you were a poem,*
I say, *a poem I wanted to show someone . . .*
and I laugh and fall dreaming again
of the desire to show you to everyone I love,
to move openly together
in the pull of gravity, which is not simple,
which carries the feathered grass a long way down the
    upbreathing air.

Adrienne Rich (b. 1929)

Put out my eyes, and I can see you still;
slam my ears to, and I can hear you yet;
and without any feet can go to you;
and tongueless, I can conjure you at will.
Break off my arms, I shall take hold of you
and grasp you with my heart as with a hand;
arrest my heart, my brain will beat as true;
and if you set this brain of mine afire,
then on my blood I yet will carry you.

Rainer Maria Rilke (1875–1926)
Translated from the German
by Babette Deutsch

Muted

Calmly in the twilight made
by the lofty boughs above,
let the silence here pervade
with profundity our love.

Let us join our souls, our senses,
and our hearts in ecstasies
among the uncertain languishments
of the pines and strawberry-trees.

Cross your arms upon your breast;
with your eyes half-closed, let dreams
from your heart that sinks to rest
chase forever all its schemes.

Let's convince ourselves, as sweet
and lulling little breezes pass,
making ripple at your feet
the russet billows of the grass.

And when from the dark oak falls
solemn evening down the air,
then will sing the nightingales,
like the voice of our despair.

Paul Verlaine (1844–1896)
Translated from the French
by C. F. MacIntyre

2195
In the Arc of Your Mallet

Don't go anywhere without me.
Let nothing happen in the sky apart from me,
or on the ground, in this world or that world,
without my being in its happening.
Vision, see nothing I don't see.
Language, say nothing.
The way the night knows itself with the moon,
be that with me. Be the rose
nearest to the thorn that I am.
I want to feel myself in you when you taste food, in the arc
of your mallet when you work.
When you visit friends, when you go
up on the roof by yourself at night.

There's nothing worse than to walk out along the street
without you. I don't know where I'm going.
You're the road and the knower of roads,
more than maps, more than love.

Rumi (1207–1273)
Translated from the Persian
by John Moyne and Coleman Barks

His Mother's Wedding Ring

The ring so worn, as you behold,
So thin, so pale, is yet of gold:
The passion such it was to prove;
Worn with life's cares, love yet was love.

George Crabbe (1754–1822)

4
from Letters from Maine

There was your voice, astonishment,
Falling into the silence suddenly
As though there were no continent
Between its warmth and me at my desk,
Bringing joy to the roots, a giant gift
Across time. Five in the morning there.
Three thousand miles to cover instantly.
How is it done? How for that matter
Did it all happen when we met?
Time telescoped, years cast away,
And primal being finding this present
Where we were lifted beyond age,
Outside responsibilities, newfound,
In a way stranded, in a way home at last?
And in your tender laughter at me
Some total acceptance of all that I am,
Of all that is to be or not ever to be
As time goes on and we are lost
Or found in it over and over again.

May Sarton (b. 1912)

Marthe Away (She Is Away)

All night I lay awake beside you,
Leaning on my elbow, watching your
Sleeping face, that face whose purity
Never ceases to astonish me.
I could not sleep. But I did not want
Sleep nor miss it. Against my body,
Your body lay like a warm soft star.
How many nights I have waked and watched
You, in how many places. Who knows?
This night might be the last one of all.
As on so many nights, once more I
Drank from your sleeping flesh the deep still
Communion I am not always strong
Enough to take from you waking, the peace of love.
Foggy lights moved over the ceiling
Of our room, so like the rooms of France
And Italy, rooms of honeymoon,
And gave your face an ever changing
Speech, the secret communication
Of untellable love. I knew then,
As your secret spoke, my secret self,
The blind bird, hardly visible in
An endless web of lies. And I knew
The web too, its every knot and strand,
The hidden crippled bird, the terrible web.

Towards the end of night, as trucks rumbled
In the streets, you stirred, cuddled to me,
And spoke my name. Your voice was the voice
Of a girl who had never known loss
Of love, betrayal, mistrust, or lie.
And later you turned again and clutched
My hand and pressed it to your body.
Now I know surely and forever,
However much I have blotted our
Waking love, its memory is still
There. And I know the web, the net,
The blind and crippled bird. For then, for
One brief instant it was not blind, nor
Trapped, nor crippled. For one heart beat the
Heart was free and moved itself. O love,
I who am lost and damned with words,
Whose words are a business and an art,
I have no words. These words, this poem, this
Is all confusion and ignorance.
But I know that coached by your sweet heart,
My heart beat one free beat and sent
Through all my flesh the blood of truth.

Kenneth Rexroth (1905–1982)

Sending Spring Love to Tzu-An

The mountain path is steep
And the stone steps dangerous,
But I do not suffer from the hardships of the journey,
But from lovesickness.
The mountain torrent that comes
From far off melting ice
Is pure as your spiritual character.
When I see the snow on the distant mountains
I think of your jade-like beauty.
Do not listen to vulgar songs
Or drink too much Spring wine
Or play chess all night with idle guests.
Steady as a pine, not like a rolling stone,
My oath of love is forever.
I long for the days
When we will be together again
Like the birds that fly
With one wing in common.
I walk alone with my regrets, longing
All day long at the end of winter
For the time when we
Will be together again under the full moon.
What can I give you as a gift of separation—
Tears that glitter in the sun on a poem.

Yü Hsüan-Chi (Mid-9th century)
Translated from the Chinese by Kenneth Rexroth and Ling Chung

The Bay of Tsunu
In the sea of Iwami
Has no fine beaches
And is not considered beautiful.
Perhaps it is not,
But we used to walk
By the sea of the whale fishers
Over the rocky shingle of Watazu
Where the wind blows
The green jewelled seaweed
Like wings quivering in the morning,
And the waves rock the kelp beds
Like wings quivering in the evening.
Just as the sea tangle sways and floats
At one with the waves,
So my girl clung to me
As she lay by my side.
Now I have left her,
To fade like the hoarfrost.
I looked back ten thousand times
At every turn of the road.
Our village fell away,
Farther and farther away.
The mountains rose between us,
Steeper and steeper.

I know she thinks of me, far off,
And wilts with longing, like summer grass.
Maybe if the mountains would bow down
I could see her again,
Standing in our doorway.

Kakinomoto No Hitomaro
(7th century)
Translated from the Japanese
by Kenneth Rexroth

Now Blue October

Now blue October, smoky in the sun,
Must end the long, sweet summer of the heart.
The last brief visit of the birds is done;
They sing the autumn songs before they part.
Listen, how lovely—there's the thrush we heard
When June was small with roses, and the bending
Blossom of branches covered nest and bird,
Singing the summer in, summer unending—
Give me your hand once more before the night;
See how the meadows darken with the frost,
How fades the green that was the summer's light.
Beauty is only altered, never lost,
And love, before the cold November rain,
Will make its summer in the heart again.

Robert Nathan (1894–1985)

Love, It Is Time

Love, it is time I memorized your phone
Number and made it part of what I keep
Not in a black book but in living bone
Of fingertips that dial you in my sleep.
Time that the Roman wires of my heart
Lead all to you like artery or vein
Or tourist roadmap or a fever chart,
Since you are central now to my love's brain.
Teri, I have your number in my blood,
Your name is red and racing in my pulse
And all my nerves are ringing as they should
Through the night's black and sweet umbilicus
Connecting our two lives with strings of words
That you send back this spring like flights of birds.

Karl Shapiro (b. 1913)

Living here
far away
I am yours
living there
far away
you are mine
love is not made
of bodies only
deep in the hearts
is where we are one

Anonymous,
Indian Sanskrit
Translated from the Sanskrit
by W. S. Merwin
and J. Moussaieff Masson

To the Tune "Glittering Sword Hilts"

I have always been sorry
Our words were so trivial
And never matched the depths
Of our thoughts. This morning
Our eyes met,
And a hundred emotions
Rushed through our veins.

Liu Yü Hsi (772–842)
Translated from the Chinese
by Kenneth Rexroth

A Dialogue of Watching

Let me celebrate you. I
Have never known anyone
More beautiful than you. I
Walking beside you, watching
You move beside me, watching
That still grace of hand and thigh,
Watching your face change with words
You do not say, watching your
Solemn eyes as thcy turn to me,
Or turn inward, full of knowing,
Slow or quick, watching your full
Lips part and smile or turn grave,
Watching your narrow waist, your
Proud buttocks in their grace, like
A sailing swan, an animal,
Free, your own, and never
To be subjugated, but
Abandoned, as I am to you,
Overhearing your perfect
Speech of motion, of love and
Trust and security as
You feed or play with our children.
I have never known any
One more beautiful than you.

Kenneth Rexroth (1905–1982)

Married Love

You and I
Have so much love,
That it
Burns like a fire,
In which we bake a lump of clay
Molded into a figure of you
And a figure of me.
Then we take both of them,
And break them into pieces,
And mix the pieces with water,
And mold again a figure of you,
And a figure of me.
I am in your clay.
You are in my clay.
In life we share a single quilt.
In death we will share one coffin.

Kuan Tao Shêng (1262–1319)
Translated from the Chinese
by Kenneth Rexroth and Ling Chung

somewhere i have never travelled,gladly beyond
any experience,your eyes have their silence:
in your most frail gesture are things which enclose me,
or which i cannot touch because they are too near

your slightest look easily will unclose me
though i have closed myself as fingers,
you open always petal by petal myself as Spring opens
(touching skilfully,mysteriously)her first rose

or if your wish be to close me,i and
my life will shut very beautifully,suddenly,
as when the heart of this flower imagines
the snow carefully everywhere descending;

nothing which we are to perceive in this world equals
the power of your intense fragility:whose texture
compels me with the colour of its countries,
rendering death and forever with each breathing

(i do not know what it is about you that closes
and opens;only something in me understands
the voice of your eyes is deeper than all roses)
nobody,not even the rain,has such small hands

e. e. cummings (1894–1962)

from XAIPE

i carry your heart with me(i carry it in
my heart)i am never without it(anywhere
i go you go,my dear;and whatever is done
by only me is your doing,my darling)
                                        i fear

no fate(for you are my fate,my sweet)i want
no world(for beautiful you are my world,my true)
and it's you are whatever a moon has always meant
and whatever a sun will always sing is you

here is the deepest secret nobody knows
(here is the root of the root and the bud of the bud
and the sky of the sky of a tree called life;which grows
higher than soul can hope or mind can hide)
and this is the wonder that's keeping the stars apart

i carry your heart(i carry it in my heart)

e. e. cummings (1894–1962)

Portrait: My Wife

"I'd rather be loved, and love, than be Shakespeare."
Ambition is what calls the mountain till it comes,
Or goes where it is and gnaws the mountain down.
But she is not ambitious. She makes a choice,
Which, being she, is forgoing neither wholly,
As: how should she not be of the many-parted poet
Miranda sometimes, Lear's daughter, or Elizabeth,
Or not be as she is, fresh beauty to the use?
She writes; is a woman; Shakespeare would know her.

As for the other, loving her makes me that poet.
Once I desired her, not seeing who she was,
Having been then married to her a morning's years,
To the straight smooth back, the opening kiss,
The laughter a red peony thrown and bursting.
She is my stranger every day. She is wretched
With doubt; everyone seeks her reassurance;
Quick-tempered as firecrackers, scornful, clean;
A spiritual materialist, Eve with clothes on.
No one knows her loneliness or believes it;
Not I, but that is the edge of my world,
And when she comes back, then I can come back
From looking over. She is warm, her cheek is warm.
Bored with sameness, we re-read one another.
We break up housekeeping to keep our house alive,
And are thought a steady pair. Oh, she has her wish!
She, whatever she does next, is my one wish.

John Holmes (1904–1962)

III
from Twenty-One Love Poems

Since we're not young, weeks have to do time
for years of missing each other. Yet only this odd warp
in time tells me we're not young.
Did I ever walk the morning streets at twenty,
my limbs streaming with a purer joy?
did I lean from any window over the city
listening for the future
as I listen here with nerves tuned for your ring?
And you, you move toward me with the same tempo.
Your eyes are everlasting, the green spark
of the blue-eyed grass of early summer,
the green-blue wild cress washed by the spring.
At twenty, yes: we thought we'd live forever.
At forty-five, I want to know even our limits.
I touch you knowing we weren't born tomorrow,
and somehow, each of us will help the other live,
and somewhere, each of us must help the other die.

Adrienne Rich (b. 1929)

The Song of Wandering Aengus

I went out to the hazel wood,
Because a fire was in my head,
And cut and peeled a hazel wand,
And hooked a berry to a thread;
And when white moths were on the wing,
And moth-like stars were flickering out,
I dropped the berry in a stream
And caught a little silver trout.

When I had laid it on the floor
I went to blow the fire a-flame,
But something rustled on the floor,
And someone called me by my name:
It had become a glimmering girl
With apple blossoms in her hair
Who called me by my name and ran
And faded through the brightening air.

Though I am old with wandering
Through hollow lands and hilly lands,
I will find out where she has gone,
And kiss her lips and take her hands;
And walk among long dappled grass,
And pluck till time and times are done
The silver apples of the moon,
The golden apples of the sun.

William Butler Yeats (1865–1939)

2674
After Being in Love, the Next Responsibility

Turn me like a waterwheel turning a millstone.
Plenty of water, Living Water.
Keep me in one place and scatter the love.
Leaf moves in a wind, straw drawn toward amber,
all parts of the world are in love,
but they do not tell their secrets: Cows grazing
on a sacramental table, ants whispering in Solomon's ear.
Mountains mumbling an echo. Sky, calm.
If the sun were not in love, he would have no brightness,
the side of the hill no grass on it.
The ocean would come to rest somewhere.

Be a lover as they are, that you come to know
your Beloved. Be faithful that you may know
Faith. The other parts of the universe did not accept
the next responsibility of love as you can.
They were afraid they might make a mistake
with it, the inspired knowing
that springs from being in love.

Rumi (1207–1273)
Translated from the Persian
by John Moyne and Coleman Barks

Geography of Music

Let me be prodigal as sun in praising you.
I take the peeping angel, frolicking
   in the branches of Time:
The dreamless churchyard on the wings
Of this gypsy moth; the face
Within the river's mist; the footsteps
Of this throbbing flower; water's rapture, leaf's
Melody in delirium of sunrise—
I take these things as factions
   in the spirit's lens
Through which I look at you. And yet,
   how can
I trust to word's furniture in moving now
Within the swarm of mountain worlds
Your lightest touch has built for me?
It is the ocean's sound of sorrowing,
It is the wonder of a thousand singing,
It is the world with all loveliness
Lost within the moons and suns of it,
Beloved, that you are.

Kenneth Patchen (1911–1972)

Madonna of the Evening Flowers

All day long I have been working,
Now I am tired.
I call: "Where are you?"
But there is only the oak tree rustling in the wind.
The house is very quiet,
The sun shines in on your books,
On your scissors and thimble just put down,
But you are not there.

Suddenly I am lonely:
Where are you?
I go about searching.
Then I see you,
Standing under a spire of pale blue larkspur,
With a basket of roses on your arm,
You are cool, like silver,
And you smile.

I think the Canterbury bells are playing little tunes.
You tell me that the peonies need spraying,
That the columbines have overrun all bounds,
That the pyrus japonica should be cut back and rounded.
You tell me these things.

But I look at you, heart of silver,
White heart-flame of polished silver,
Burning beneath the blue steeples of the larkspur,
And I long to kneel instantly at your feet,
While all about us peal the loud, sweet *Te Deums* of the
    Canterbury bells.

Amy Lowell (1874–1925)

Ratio

Thinking about you
is to being with you
as the state of coma
is to waking wide,
as a particle second
is to an hour
raised to the highest
possible power.

Lillian Morrison
(b. 1917)

Like the tides' flood
In Izumo Bay,
Ever deeper and deeper
Grows my love,
Each time I think of you.

Anonymous, Japanese
(Quoted in 10th century
and referred to as a very
old folksong)
Translated from the Japanese
by Kenneth Rexroth

So small are the flowers of Seamu
Whoever looks at them feels a giant.

I am the first among your loves,
Like a freshly sprinkled garden of grass and perfumed
    flowers.

Pleasant is the channel you have dug
In the freshness of the north wind.

Tranquil our paths
When your hand rests on mine in joy.

Your voice gives life, like nectar.

To see you, is more than food or drink.

Anonymous, Egyptian hieroglyphic text (c. 1500–1000 B.C.)
Translated by Ezra Pound and Noel Stock from the literal translation of the
hieroglyphic text into Italian by Boris de Rachewiltz

Take from my palms, to soothe your heart,
a little honey, a little sun,
in obedience to Persephone's bees.

You can't untie a boat that was never moored,
nor hear a shadow in its furs,
nor move through thick life without fear.

For us, all that's left is kisses
tattered as the little bees
that die when they leave the hive.

Deep in the transparent night they're still humming,
at home in the dark wood on the mountain,
in the mint and lungwort and the past.

But lay to your heart my rough gift,
this unlovely dry necklace of dead bees
that once made a sun out of honey.

Osip Mandelstam (1891–1938)
Translated from the Russian
by Clarence Brown and W. S. Merwin

Degli Sposi

Of us
not much is known.
Our lives were not
extraordinary.
Our silence seals
a deeper silence.

Sharing the single bed, how close
we lie; fingers curved over palms
whose fable reads: *conjugal bliss
is possible*.

How simple it was. It is.
But the secret's lost. That's why
you look to us, how we carry
ourselves, our smile. We live
in that space where all's yet
to become: embrace—a tenderness,
an expectation, myth, tentative
gesture preceding touch. Before
the shock of contact, when caution
counsels: Leave.

Not at all easy, this, to speak
of love. And to survive. Our skin
glows red with passion in reserve.
Unbridled, it would deaden every
nerve. Feeling—the reins, the check,
restraint, repose, out of whose thousand
fragments we are restored. Loving
each other even after death. As if
life were not, had not been, enough.

We touch, we hold, we keep
one another free.

Rika Lesser (b. 1953)

Degli Sposi means "of the married"—a married couple.

Love Story
(for Deirdre)

You keep our love hidden
like the nightdress you keep under your pillow
and never wear when I'm there

But
one sunfilled day
you took me to your magic room
at the end of the yellow corridor
and showed me enchanted still-lifes
Niveatins . . . BodyMist sprays coldcream jars
glowing like jewels
your body singing pink in the sunlight
opening to me like the red pulsing heart of a flower
in Public Gardens
where peacocks open their thousand eyes for us
and birdpeople move noiselessly
through the dripping palmhouse
feeling your body under me
warm and alive as the grass under our feet

I LOVE YOU
When listening to Bruckner in the sunlit bathroom
When the hills and valleys of your morning body
are hidden from my gaze by BodyMist
When I don't have to ask who it is on the telephone
When we can't wait till the programme finishes

When I slip out quietly leaving you to sleep
untroubled dreams till morning in your darkened room
When I walk out into the dark shining streets
bright signs from petrolstations lamplight on leaves
hard unyielding lights from city flats

I LOVE YOU
Walking home yellow moon over the rooftops
cars crawling girls stopping everywhere smelling of you
Going off to sleep still smelling the rich luxury lather
    in your hair
Walking holding your mini-hand
Standing in the Saturdaymorning bank
Hot with people worrying about money
Seeing half a bottle of gin smashed on the pavement
Even when seeing schoolgirls on buses
their blackstocking knees in mourning for their lost
    virginity

I LOVE YOU
On trains
in cars
on buses
in taxis

I LOVE YOU
in that midnight hour
when all the clocks stopped
and it was midsummer
forever.

                                    Adrian Henri (b. 1932)

Woman

When you were a girl
you could sting
like the thorn of a wild blackberry.
Your foot, too, little savage,
you wielded as a weapon.

You were hard to take.

                        Now still young
You are still lovely, the threads
of years and sorrow bind together
our souls, and make them one. No longer
under the jet-black strands that my fingers
gather in do I fear
the little white faunlike keen-pointed ear.

Umberto Saba (1883–1957)
Translated from the Italian
by Thomas G. Bergin

The White Birds

I would that we were, my beloved, white birds on the foam
    of the sea:
We tire of the flame of the meteor, before it can pass by
    and flee;
And the flame of the blue star of twilight, hung low on the
    rim of the sky,
Has awaked in our hearts, my beloved, a sadness that may
    never die.

A weariness comes from those dreamers, dew-dabbled, the
    lily and rose,
Ah, dream not of them, my beloved, the flame of the
    meteor that goes,
Or the flame of the blue star that lingers hung low in the
    fall of the dew:
For I would we were changed to white birds on the
    wandering foam: I and you.

I am haunted by numberless islands, and many a
    Danaan shore,
Where Time would surely forget us, and Sorrow come
    near us no more:
Soon far from the rose and the lily, the fret of the flames,
    would we be,
Were we only white birds, my beloved, buoyed out on the
    foam of the sea.

William Butler Yeats (1865–1939)

I Hid You

I hid you for a long time
the way a branch hides its
slowly ripening fruit among leaves,
and like a flower of sane ice
on a window
you open in my mind.
Now I know what it means
when your hand swoops up to your hair.
In my heart I keep
the small tilt of your ankle too
and I'm amazed by the delicate curve
of your ribs, coldly
like someone who has lived
such breathing miracles.
Still, in my dreams
I often have a hundred arms
and like God in a dream
I hold you in those arms.

Miklós Radnóti (1908–1944)
Translated from the Hungarian
by Steven Polgar, Stephen Berg, and S. J. Marks

An interesting note on the poem—and its title. Radnóti was a prisoner in a Nazi labor brigade. In late fall of 1944, he and 21 of his companions were taken on a forced march (in Yugoslavia near the Bor concentration camp), shot, and buried in a mass grave. When the corpses were exhumed, a small notebook of poems was found in his jacket pocket.

XIV
from is 5 part IV

it is so long since my heart has been with yours

shut by our mingling arms through
a darkness where new lights begin and
increase,
since your mind has walked into
my kiss as a stranger
into the streets and colours of a town—

that i have perhaps forgotten
how,always(from
these hurrying crudities
of blood and flesh)Love
coins His most gradual gesture,

and whittles life to eternity

—after which our separating selves become museums
filled with skilfully stuffed memories

e. e. cummings (1894–1962)

A Sprig of Rosemary

I cannot see your face.
When I think of you,
It is your hands which I see.
Your hands
Sewing,
Holding a book,
Resting for a moment on the sill of a window.
My eyes keep always the sight of your hands,
But my heart holds the sound of your voice,
And the soft brightness which is your soul.

Amy Lowell (1874–1925)

558

They try to say what you are, spiritual or sexual?
They wonder about Solomon and all his wives.

In the body of the world, they say, there is a Soul
and you are *that*.

But we have ways within each other
that will never be said by anyone.

Rumi (1207–1273)

Translated from the Persian
by John Moyne and Coleman Barks

1246

The minute I heard my first love story
I started looking for you, not knowing
how blind that was.

Lovers don't finally meet somewhere.
They're in each other all along.

Rumi (1207–1273)
Translated from the Persian
by John Moyne and Coleman Barks

The Snow Is Deep on the Ground

The snow is deep on the ground.
Always the light falls
Softly down on the hair of my belovèd.

This is a good world.
The war has failed.
God shall not forget us.
Who made the snow waits where love is.

Only a few go mad.
The sky moves in its whiteness
Like the withered hand of an old king.
God shall not forget us.
Who made the sky knows of our love.

The snow is beautiful on the ground.
And always the lights of heaven glow
Softly down on the hair of my belovèd.

Kenneth Patchen (1911–1972)

No, Love Is Not Dead

No, love is not dead in this heart and these eyes and this mouth that proclaimed the beginning of its own requiem.

Listen, I've had enough of the picturesque, of colors and charm.

I love love, its tenderness and its cruelty.

The one I love has only a single name, a single form.

Everything goes. Mouths cling to this mouth.

The one I love has only one name, one form.

And some day if you remember it

O you, form and name of my love,

One day on the sea between America and Europe,

When the last ray of sun flashes on the undulating surface of the waves, or else one stormy night beneath a tree in the country, or in a speeding car,

One spring morning Boulevard Malesherbes,

One rainy day,

At dawn before putting yourself to bed,

Tell yourself, I summon your familiar ghost, that I was the only one to love you more and what a pity it is you didn't know it.

Tell yourself you shouldn't be sorry for anything: before me Ronsard and Baudelaire sang the sorrows of old women and dead women who despised the purest love.

You, when you die,

You will still be beautiful and desirable.

I'll already be dead, completely enclosed in your immortal body, in your astonishing image present forever among the perpetual wonders of life and eternity, but if I outlive you

Your voice and how it sounds, your gaze and how it shines,

The smell of you and of your hair and many other things will still go on living in me,

In me, and I'm no Ronsard or Baudelaire,

Just me Robert Desnos who, for having known and loved you,

Is as good as they are.

Just me Robert Desnos who, for loving you

Doesn't want to be remembered for anything else on this despicable earth.

Robert Desnos (1900–1945)
Translated from the French
by Bill Zavatsky

Nocturne

If the deep wood is haunted, it is I
Who am the ghost; not the tall trees
Nor the white moonlight slanting down like rain,
Filling the hollows with bright pools of silver.

A long train whistle serpentines around the hill
Now shrill, now far away.
Tell me, from what dark smoky terminal
What train sets out for yesterday?

Or, since our spirits take off and resume
Their flesh as travellers their cloaks, O tell me where,
In what age and what country you will come,
That I may meet you there.

Robert Hillyer (1895–1961)

In Judgment of the Leaf

And we were speaking easily and all the light stayed low
Within your eyes; I think no equal glass has since been
    ground.
My love was looking through the throng that gave you
    mind.

We were quiet as the stars began to ride the billows;
And watching them we took an only mortal stair.
We wandered up the stable rays, were startled, lost
In a child's land whose stars are glory of jangling buoys,
Gunned by the froth of eternity and space.

    Something snapped a twig at a distance from us:
    it seemed real: a bird called its little bonfire of sound:
    thickets flamed with the trial of a leaf in the night

Gentle hands were warm, scared within my hands; the
    moment's
Church wavered through Time's dripping tapers . . . was
    torn away.

    Suddenly
We knew that we could not belong again to simple love.
I saw your opening eyes reject the trade of tiny things
And I reasoned that the whole world might lie naked
In the earth of your eyes, in easy wonder building God.

Kenneth Patchen (1911–1972)

being to timelessness as it's to time,
love did no more begin than love will end;
where nothing is to breathe to stroll to swim
love is the air the ocean and the land

(do lovers suffer?all divinities
proudly descending put on deathful flesh:
are lovers glad?only their smallest joy's
a universe emerging from a wish)

love is the voice under all silences,
the hope which has no opposite in fear;
the strength so strong mere force is feebleness:
the truth more first than sun more last than star

—do lovers love?why then to heaven with hell.
Whatever sages say and fools, all's well

e. e. cummings (1894—1962)

INDEX OF AUTHORS

INDEX OF TITLES

INDEX OF FIRST LINES